THE One & Only soups Cookbook

THE One & Only soups Cookbook

All the recipes you will ever need

With a foreword by
Jenny Linford

WeldonOwen
PUBLISHING

WeldonOwen
PUBLISHING

First published in the UK by
Weldon Owen Ltd., an imprint of the Bonnier Group
The Plaza
535 King's Road
London
SW10 0SZ
www.weldonowen.co.uk
www.bonnierpublishing.com

ISBN-13: 978 1 78342 217 3

A catalogue record for this book is available from the
British Library

Printed and bound by Interak, Poland
10 9 8 7 6 5 4 3 2 1

"Anyone who tells a lie
has not a pure heart, and cannot make
a good soup."

Ludwig van Beethoven

Contents

Foreword

By Jenny Linford

Soup is one of those fundamental dishes, existing as a staple in cuisines around the world. As the recipes in this book demonstrate, it is a supremely versatile dish, existing in numerous forms: hot or cold, savoury or sweet, thick or thin, served as a canapé, starter or main meal. Soup can be heartening and homely or light and elegant. Once you've learnt the basic principles of making soup, you can enjoy experimenting.

The importance of stock

Using a good-quality stock as your starting point is the secret to making excellent soup. As with soups, stocks range widely, from Japanese 'dashi' made from dried bonito and kelp, to French veal stock. Cooks in a hurry can buy stock cubes or granules and tubs of ready-made stock, but the best and most economical results are to be had by making your own stock, a simple process which requires time but very little attention.

Bones are the starting point for a good meat or chicken stock, with butchers shops a useful source of stock bones. Alternately, cheap cuts of meat on the bone, such as chicken wings, are ideal for stock-making. Do remember, too, never to waste a roast chicken carcase; instead, use it to make stock.

How to make a good stock

When making a meat or chicken stock, the best flavour is achieved by using chopped fresh vegetables, fresh herbs and spices in addition to bones. Classic additions to the stock-pot in Western cuisines are carrots, onions, celery, leeks, fresh parsley, bay leaves and peppercorns, while in China spring onions, garlic cloves and ginger are popular. The bones can either be cooked from raw, making 'white' stock, or roasted beforehand to create 'brown' stock.

To make meat or chicken stock, simply place the a generous quantity of bones, vegetables and herbs in a saucepan, add cold water to cover, bring to the boil, skim off any scum, reduce the heat so that the stock is simmering very gently, partly cover and cook for 2 hours. The more gently the stock is simmered the clearer it will be. Strain through a fine sieve. If not using immediately, cool, refrigerate and use within 3 days.

Make vegetable stock from chopped, fresh vegetables such as carrots, onion, celery and fennel - either using them raw or frying them beforehand - plus herbs such as parsley and bay. Place the vegetables and herbs in a saucepan, cover with cold water, bring to the boil, then reduce the heat and simmer for 40 minutes. Strain the stock through a fine sieve and use as required.

Fish stock is made from fish heads, bones and trimmings, while seafood stock can be made from prawn heads and shells, crab or lobster shells. In European cookery, a little dry white wine is often added when making fish stock. Cover the bones, vegetables and herbs with water, bring to the boil, skim off any scum and simmer for 20 minutes. Don't be tempted to simmer fish stock for longer as the stock will simply become bitter and slightly gluey.

Creating texture

Soups range from fine, clear broths to thick creations and adjusting their texture is part of the fun of making them. Give body to your soup by adding in ingredients such as diced vegetables, small pasta shapes or a handful of rice. One simple way to produce a smooth but thick-textured soup is to cook the ingredients – say leek and potato – in the stock until tender, then blend the soup using a hand blender, food processor or jug blender. For extra, velvety smoothness, pass the blended soup through a fine-meshed sieve.

Finishing touches

Both visually and texturally, garnishes are a simple but effective way to give your soup that little extra lift. Sprinkling over finely chopped herbs, such as chives, dill or parsley adds a fresh note. An appealing crunch can be added by adding garnishes such as crudités (made from fried, cubed bread), roasted pumpkin seeds, crispy deep-fried shallots or finely chopped cucumber or red pepper.

A touch of contrasting colour and flavour is another great way to finish off your soup, so a white swirl of soured cream on top of a beetroot soup, a spoonful of creamy yoghurt with spiced lentils or a drizzle of deep green olive oil over minestrone.

Caramelised parsnip soup

1. Heat the oven to 400°F (200°C). Heat the butter in an ovenproof dish or roasting tin and add the parsnips and sprigs of thyme. Turn to coat in the butter. Roast in the oven for about 30–35 minutes, stirring once, until golden brown. Stir in the honey and cook for a further 10 minutes until the parsnips have caramelised.

2. Remove the dish from the oven, add the stock and bring it to a boil on top of the hob. Reduce the heat and simmer for 10 minutes.

3. Carefully pour the soup into a blender or food processor and purée until smooth. Season to taste, return to the pan and stir in 300ml boiling water. Bring back to a boil.

4. Stir in the cream and parsley and gently heat through. Divide between bowls and garnish with parsnip crisps, a few thyme leaves and ground black pepper. Serve with chunks of crusty bread.

Preparation time: 10 min
Cooking time: 50 min
Serves 4–6

25g unsalted butter
750g parsnips, peeled and roughly chopped
2 sprigs fresh thyme
2 tbsp honey
1 litre chicken or vegetable stock
Salt and pepper to season
60ml double cream
2 tbsp freshly chopped flat-leaf parsley
parsnip crisps, to serve
ground black pepper, to serve
fresh thyme leaves, to serve

Moroccan chickpea and chicken soup

1. Heat the oil in a large saucepan and cook the onion and garlic until softened. Stir in the ground spices and cook for 1–2 minutes, then add the chickpeas, stock and tomatoes and season well.

2. Simmer, uncovered, for 8–10 minutes. Stir in the chicken, lemon juice and harissa paste. Cook for 2–3 minutes until the chicken is heated through. Serve in bowls, topped with the lemon zest and fresh herbs. Serve with griddled flat breads.

Preparation time: 5 min
Cooking time: 15 min
Serves 4

2 tbsp oil
1 onion, chopped
1 garlic clove, crushed
1 tsp ground cumin
1 tsp ground coriander
1 tsp ground cinnamon
400g tin chickpeas, drained
600ml chicken stock
400g tin chopped tomatoes
200g cooked chicken, shredded
grated zest and juice of ½ a lemon
2 tsp harissa paste
2 tbsp freshly chopped flat-leaf parsley
2 tbsp freshly chopped coriander
flat breads, to serve

Oriental miso noodle soup

1. Pour 1 litre of boiling water into a large pan and return to boil. Add the miso paste, seaweed, ginger and spring onions.

2. Break the pak choi into individual leaves and add to the pan. Cover and simmer for 2–3 minutes until it is beginning to wilt.

3. Add the noodles and tofu. Simmer for 2–3 minutes until the noodles are tender.

4. Pour the soup into bowls, and serve garnished with the chilli and coriander leaves.

Preparation time: 5 min
Cooking time: 10 min
Serves 4

3 tbsp miso paste
1 tbsp dried wakame seaweed, crumbled
2.5cm piece fresh root ginger, peeled and thinly sliced
bunch spring onions, sliced
250g pak choi
125g rice noodles
225g firm silken style tofu, cut into small cubes
1 red chilli, deseeded and finely sliced, to serve
fresh coriander leaves, to serve

Pea, feta and mint soup

Preparation time: 10 min
Cooking time: 25 min
Serves 4

50g butter
1 small onion, finely chopped
250g floury potatoes, peeled
  and diced
1 litre hot vegetable stock
450g frozen peas
4 tbsp freshly chopped mint, plus a
  few whole ones to serve
100g feta cheese, crumbled

1. Melt the butter in a large pan. Add the onion and fry gently for 5 minutes, or until softened. Add the potatoes and stir well. Cover and cook for 5 minutes.

2. Pour in the stock, season, and bring to a boil. Cover and simmer for 12–15 minutes, or until the potatoes are tender.

3. Stir in the peas and cook for 3 minutes, or until just tender. Pour the soup in batches into a food processor or blender and process until smooth.

4. Return the soup to the pan and reheat gently. Stir in the mint and season to taste.

5. Ladle the soup into bowls and sprinkle with the feta. Garnish with mint leaves.

Potato and chorizo soup

1. Finely slice about a quarter of the chorizo and chop the remainder. Heat the oil in a large saucepan, and add the sliced chorizo. Cook over a moderate heat until crisp. Remove, drain on kitchen paper and reserve for garnish.

2. Add the onion and remaining chorizo to the pan and cook until softened, stirring occasionally. Stir in the potatoes, cover and cook for 5 minutes.

3. Stir in the stock. Cover and simmer for 35–40 minutes until the potatoes are tender. Transfer to a food processor or liquidiser and blend in batches until smooth. Return to the pan and reheat gently. Season to taste.

4. Serve with a spoonful of Greek yoghurt, garnished with a few slices of the chorizo and a sprinkling of chives.

Preparation time: 10 min
Cooking time: 50 min
Serves 4

125g chorizo
1 tbsp olive oil
1 large onion, sliced
300g potato, peeled and chopped
300g sweet potato, peeled and chopped
900ml chicken stock
4 tbsp Greek yoghurt, to serve
2 tbsp freshly chopped chives, to serve

Creamed venison and mushroom soup

1. Heat the oil in a large pan and add the venison pieces. Brown on all sides (you may need to do this in batches). Remove the meat from the pan and set aside.

2. Gently cook the bacon in the pan until the fat starts to run then add the onion, carrot and garlic and cook gently until the vegetables are soft.

3. Sprinkle over the flour, cook for 1 minute then gradually add the stock, wine, bay leaves and thyme, bring to the boil, season with salt and pepper and simmer for 30 minutes.

4. Heat the butter in a frying pan and gently add the ceps and chanterelles. Cook until lightly browned and transfer them to the pan with the venison. Cook for 15 more minutes. In the same pan, add the bread cubes and fry until golden brown.

5. Stir the cream into the soup and check the seasoning. Serve with the fried bread scattered over and a dollop of sour cream on top.

Preparation time: 10 min
Cooking time: 1 h
Serves 4

3 tbsp oil
450g venison steaks, diced
2 rashers bacon, chopped
1 onion, finely chopped
1 carrot, finely chopped
1 garlic clove, chopped
1 tbsp flour
750ml venison or beef stock
250ml white wine
2 bay leaves
2 tsp dried thyme
salt and pepper to taste
2 tbsp butter
150g fresh ceps, cleaned and
    chopped
150g fresh chanterelles, cleaned and
    chopped
2 slices stale white bread, diced
250ml double cream
4 tsp sour cream, to serve

Spicy chicken, potato and leek soup

1. Place the chicken in a wide pan with the stock or water and bring to a boil. Simmer very gently for 15 minutes or until the chicken is cooked through. Remove from the heat, shred the meat and reserve the liquid.

2. Heat the butter in a clean pan and gently add the leek. Cook until soft but not brown. Add the garlic, chilli and potatoes. Cook for 2 minutes. Pour over the reserved stock.

3. Bring to a boil and simmer gently until the potatoes are very soft. Slightly mash the soup with a fork or potato masher.

4. Add the cream, season with salt and pepper and reheat gently. Serve in warmed bowls with the shredded chicken on top.

Preparation time: 10 min
Cooking time: 30 min
Serves 4

2 chicken breasts, skinned
750ml chicken stock or water
3 tbsp butter
1 leek, chopped
1 garlic clove, chopped
1 red chilli pepper, deseeded and
   finely chopped
2 medium potatoes, peeled
   and chopped
125ml double cream

Spicy scallop and potato soup

Preparation time: 10 min
Cooking time: 20 min
Serves 4

3 tbsp olive oil
1 medium leek, finely chopped
2 medium potatoes, peeled
   and diced
1 stalk lemongrass
1 red chilli pepper, deseeded and
   sliced
750ml fish stock
1 ½ tbsp fish sauce
2 tbsp butter
8 scallops
coriander leaves, to garnish

1. Heat the oil in a large pan and gently cook the leek until it is soft but not brown.

2. Add the potatoes and cook for 2 minutes, stirring from time to time. Remove the outer leaves from the lemongrass, chop the tender leaves and add to the pan with the chilli.

3. Stir for 1 minute. Add the stock and fish sauce. Bring to a boil and simmer for about 15 minutes, until the potatoes are cooked. Season to taste with salt and pepper.

4. Meanwhile, heat the butter in a large frying pan and quickly fry the scallops for about 1 minute each side. Remove and cool slightly. Slice in half horizontally, add to the hot soup and reheat for about 10 seconds. Ladle the soup into deep plates and garnish with coriander.

Potato and bean soup

1. Drain the soaked butterbeans, rinse well and place in a large pan with the onion, parsley, carrots, celery and bay leaf. Add about 1.2 litres water and bring to the boil. Simmer gently for about 1 hour or until the beans are tender. Drain the beans, reserving the liquid, and discard the onion, parsley, carrots and bay leaf.

2. Heat the vegetable oil in a large pan and gently cook the garlic until softened. Add the potatoes, sage and rosemary, cook for 2 minutes then pour over the bean liquid. Set aside about a fifth of the beans and add the remainder to the pan.

3. Bring to the boil and simmer for about 20 minutes or until the potatoes are very tender. Meanwhile, mix together the parsley, basil, olive oil and Parmesan and set aside.

4. Blend the soup until smooth, then add the reserved beans and reheat gently. Add the lemon juice and season with salt and pepper.

5. Serve the soup with the parsley and basil mixture drizzled over.

Preparation time: 10 min
  plus overnight soaking
Cooking time: 1 h 25 min
Serves 4

*200g dried butterbeans (lima beans),
  soaked overnight
1 onion, roughly chopped
2 sprigs parsley
2 carrots, roughly chopped
1 stalk celery, roughly chopped
1 bay leaf
2 tbsp vegetable oil
2 garlic cloves, chopped
2 large potatoes, roughly chopped
2 tsp chopped sage leaves
1 tsp chopped rosemary leaves
juice of ½ lemon*

*For the drizzle:
1 tbsp finely chopped parsley
1 tbsp finely chopped basil
2 tbsp olive oil
1 tbsp grated Parmesan*

Creamed lettuce soup

1. Wash the lettuce, shake dry and chop into thin strips.

2. Heat the butter in a pan and gently cook the onion until soft but not brown. Sprinkle over the flour and cook for 2 minutes, stirring all the time.

3. Add the stock and simmer for 10–15 minutes, stirring occasionally. Reserve 4 tablespoons of lettuce strips and add the rest to the soup. Add the cream and season well with salt, pepper, nutmeg and lemon juice.

4. Simmer for a further 5 minutes. Blend the soup until smooth and adjust the seasoning. Serve the soup on plates or in bowls garnished with the reserved lettuce strips and chives.

Preparation time: 10 min
Cooking time: 25 min
Serves 4

2 soft lettuces
2 tbsp butter
1 onion, finely chopped
1 tbsp flour
750ml chicken stock
200ml double cream
pinch of grated nutmeg
juice of ½ lemon
snipped chives, to serve

Potato soup with salmon caviar and crème fraîche

1. Heat the oil in a large pan, add the onion and cook until soft but not brown.

2. Add the garlic and turmeric, cook for 2 minutes. Add the potatoes and carrots and cook for 2 more minutes.

3. Pour over the stock. Bring to a boil, then simmer gently until the vegetables are very soft. Blend to a smooth purée. Pass through a fine sieve into a clean pan.

4. Add the cream to the pan, season with salt and pepper and reheat gently. Pour into warmed bowls and garnish with the chives, caviar and crème fraîche.

Preparation time: 10 min
Cooking time: 30 min
Serves 4

3 tbsp vegetable oil
1 onion, chopped
1 garlic clove, chopped
1 tsp ground turmeric
2 medium potatoes, peeled
  and chopped
2 carrots, peeled and chopped
750ml vegetable stock
250ml double cream

To serve:
2 tbsp snipped chives
4 tbsp salmon caviar
4 tbsp crème fraîche

Spicy chestnut soup

1. Heat the oil in a large pan. Add the bacon and onion and gently fry until soft but not brown.

2. Add the garlic and paprika and cook for 1 minute. Drain and rinse the chestnuts. Roughly chop about 8 and finely chop the rest.

3. Add the finely chopped chestnuts to the pan with the tomatoes, red wine and stock and simmer gently for about 15 minutes. Add the parsley, rosemary, balsamic vinegar, tomato purée and the sugar. Cook for 5 more minutes then season with salt and pepper.

4. Meanwhile, melt the butter in a small pan and gently cook the mushrooms until soft. Add the roughly chopped chestnuts and cook until browned.

5. Garnish with the mushroom and chestnut mixture.

Preparation time: 10 min
Cooking time: 30 min
Serves 4

2 tbsp olive oil
2 rashers bacon, finely chopped
1 onion, finely chopped
1 garlic clove, chopped
1 tsp paprika
200g chestnuts, tinned
200g tomatoes, skinned, deseeded
 and chopped
200ml red wine
600ml vegetable stock
1 tbsp chopped parsley
1 tbsp chopped rosemary
1 tbsp balsamic vinegar
1 tbsp tomato purée
1 tbsp sugar
2 tbsp butter
100g button mushrooms,
 roughly chopped

Chive cream soup

1. Wash and sort the chives and shake dry. Chop into 3cm lengths.

2. Melt the butter in a pan and gently cook the shallots until soft but not brown. Add the flour, cook for 2 minutes, stirring all the time, then gradually add the stock.

3. Bring to a boil and simmer gently for 10 minutes. Add the cream and heat through. Add three-quarters of the chives and remove from the heat.

4. Blend to make a smooth soup. Pass through a fine sieve and season with salt and pepper. Garnish with the remaining chives.

Preparation time: 8 min
Cooking time: 12 min
Serves 4

100g chives
2 tbsp butter
2 shallots, finely chopped
1 tbsp flour
750ml vegetable stock
100ml double cream

Lemon chicken soup

Preparation time: 10 min
Cooking time: 25 min
Serves 4

*4 stalks lemongrass, outer leaves
  removed and inner leaves cut
  into thin strips*
2 lime leaves
*thumb-size piece fresh ginger,
  peeled and chopped*
*1 red chilli pepper, deseeded
  and sliced*
1 litre chicken stock
2 chicken breasts, skinned
100g chestnut mushrooms, sliced
100g shiitake mushrooms, sliced
juice of 1 lime
2 tbsp fish sauce
1 tsp sugar
coriander leaves, to serve

1. Place the lemongrass, lime leaves, ginger and chilli in a large pan. Add the chicken stock. Bring to a boil and simmer gently for 10 minutes.

2. Add the chicken breast and simmer for 5 more minutes. Remove the chicken from the pan and slice into strips.

3. Add the mushrooms to the pan. Simmer very gently for 5 minutes and add the chicken strips, lime juice, fish sauce and sugar and heat through. Season with salt and pepper and garnish with the coriander.

Cream of chanterelle soup with marjoram

1. Clean the chanterelles thoroughly using a small brush.

2. Heat the butter and oil in a pan. Add the spring onions and chanterelles and cook until soft.

3. Remove about one-third of the chanterelle mixture and set aside. With the remaining mixture left in, deglaze the pan with the white wine and boil to reduce slightly. Add the stock and simmer gently for 5 minutes. Stir in the cream and season with salt and pepper.

4. Mix the cornflour with about 2 tablespoons cold water and add to the pan, stirring well. Blend the soup until smooth and pass through a fine sieve into a clean pan. Gently reheat, stir in the remaining chanterelle mixture and garnish with the marjoram.

Preparation time: 15 min
Cooking time: 25 min
Serves 4

450g fresh chanterelles
3 tbsp butter
1 tsp olive oil
4 spring onions, sliced
100ml white wine
800ml vegetable stock
125ml double cream
1 tbsp cornflour
a few fresh marjoram leaves,
  to serve

Cold cucumber soup with smoked salmon and sour cream

1. Place the cucumbers, garlic, spring onions and water in a food processor or blender and purée until smooth.

2. Place in a bowl and add the mustard, lemon juice, sugar, cumin and dill. Season with salt and pepper and chill for at least 2 hours.

3. Serve with a swirl of sour cream, the smoked salmon and dill scattered over and a grinding of black pepper.

Preparation time: 15 min
  plus 2 h chilling
Serves 4

2 cucumbers, seeds removed and
  flesh chopped
1 garlic clove, chopped
2 spring onions, finely chopped
250ml cold water
1 tsp Dijon mustard
3–4 tbsp lemon juice
1 tsp sugar
1 tsp ground cumin
3 tbsp dill, roughly chopped

To serve:
4 tsp sour cream
50g smoked salmon, cut into strips
4 sprigs dill

French onion soup with cheese toasts

1. Heat the butter and oil in a large pan. Add the onions and some salt.

2. Cook over a very gentle heat, stirring from time to time, for about 20 minutes. Add the wine, stock, thyme and bay leaf and simmer for 30 minutes.

3. Season with salt and pepper and remove the thyme and bay leaf. Blend to make a smooth soup. Return to the pan and reheat gently.

4. Heat the grill to High and grill the bread on one side. Turn the bread over and place some grated cheese on the top of each slice, setting aside a handful for the serving. Grill until all the cheese has just melted.

5. Pour the soup in warmed bowls. Top each with a cheese toast and scatter over the remaining cheese.

Preparation time: 10 min
Cooking time: 1 h
Serves 6

3 tbsp butter
1 tbsp vegetable oil
6 large onions, roughly chopped
1 tsp salt
125ml white wine
1.2 litres chicken stock
6 sprigs fresh thyme, tied with
*   kitchen twine*
1 bay leaf

For cheese toasts:
6 slices French bread
200g Gruyère cheese, grated

Leek, lemon and marjoram soup

Preparation time: 5 min
Cooking time: 35 min
Serves 4

900g leeks, cleaned and finely
   sliced
3 tbsp olive oil
1 onion, chopped
2 garlic cloves, chopped
4 tsp chopped marjoram leaves
100ml dry white wine
1 litre vegetable stock
zest and juice of 1 lemon
2 tbsp double cream
grated nutmeg
marjoram sprigs, to serve

1. Set aside a few slices of leek to garnish the soup. Heat the oil in a pan. Add the onion and the remaining leek and cook until they start to soften.

2. Add the garlic and marjoram and cook gently for 10 minutes, stirring from time to time.

3. Add the wine and stock. Bring to the boil, cover and simmer for about 20 minutes. Remove from the heat and blend to a purée.

4. Return the soup to the pan and reheat gently. Stir in the lemon juice and season with salt and pepper. Serve in warmed bowls with a drizzle of cream, the reserved leeks, lemon zest, nutmeg and marjoram.

Minestrone with pesto

1. Place the tomatoes in boiling water for a few seconds, then immediately plunge them into cold water. Peel the tomatoes and chop them in half. Remove the seeds and chop the flesh.

2. Bring about 1 litre of water to a boil. Add all vegetables and pour in the olive oil. Season with salt and pepper. Bring to a boil again and reduce the heat. Cover and simmer for 30 minutes. Add the pasta and cook the soup until the pasta is tender and crisp.

3. Season the soup with salt and pepper and ladle into soup bowls. Spoon a little pesto on the top.

Preparation time: 15 min
Cooking time: 45 min
Serves 4

4 large tomatoes
2 carrots, finely chopped
2 courgettes, finely chopped
1 fennel bulb, finely chopped
1 onion, finely chopped
2 medium potatoes, peeled
*   and chopped*
3 tbsp olive oil
150g small pasta shapes
2 tbsp pesto

Mussel soup with pastis and tarragon

1. Wash the mussels well in cold water. Remove the beards and discard any mussels that remain open when tapped.

2. Put about 500ml water into a pan with the wine, pastis and bay leaves and bring to a boil. Add the mussels and cover with a lid. After 3 minutes, remove the cooked mussels from the pan with a slotted spoon, discarding any that have not opened. Set aside.

3. Add the fennel to the pan and simmer for about 10 minutes. Add the cream and return to a boil. Add the mustard and return the mussels to the pan.

4. Season with salt and pepper, gently reheat and garnish with the tarragon.

Preparation time: 15 min
Cooking time: 20 min
Serves 4

1.35kg mussels
250ml white wine
3 tbsp pastis
2 bay leaves
1 small fennel bulb, finely chopped
250ml double cream
1 tsp mustard
sprigs tarragon

STEP 1 Cut off the top of the unpeeled onion using a sharp knife to create a flat surface.

How to chop an onion

Chopping an onion is one of the most common kitchen tasks, but the neatest, easiest way to accomplish it isn't the most obvious. This technique is safe and also works for garlic and shallots.

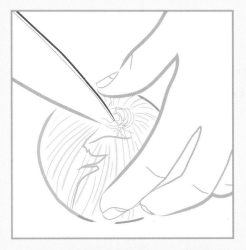

STEP 2 Position the onion on a chopping board on its flat end, then, with a sharp knife, cut it in half through the root. Peel the skin off both halves.

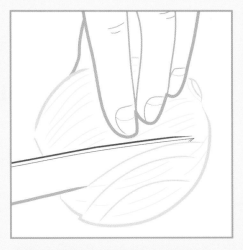

STEP 3 Holding the onion firmly with your fingertips, make evenly spaced vertical cuts into the sides of the onion, stopping short of the root end.

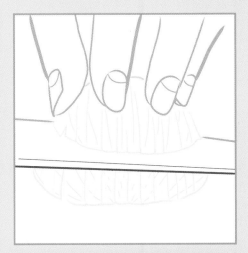

STEP 4 Turn the onion and, holding it tight across the vertical cuts, carefully slice horizontally, again just stopping short of the root.

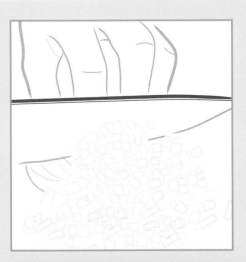

STEP 5 Slice the onion across the vertical cuts, letting the diced pieces fall away. Repeat the process with the second half of the onion.

Salmon and leek soup

1. Heat the butter in a large pan. Add the leeks and gently cook until soft. Add the potatoes, stir for 2 minutes and pour over the stock.

2. Bring to a boil. Simmer gently for about 20 minutes until the potatoes are soft.

3. Meanwhile, heat the oil in a frying pan. Add the pancetta or bacon and cook the pancetta until crisp. Drain on kitchen paper and set aside.

4. When the potatoes are soft, add the salmon to the pan and simmer very gently for about 3 minutes or until the salmon is just cooked.

5. Stir in the cream, dill and lemon juice. Season with salt and pepper and reheat very gently.

6. Serve the soup in warmed bowls with the crisp pancetta and parsley scattered over.

Preparation time: 10 min
Cooking time: 30 min
Serves 4

2 tbsp butter
1 leek, finely sliced
2 large potatoes, finely diced
750ml fish or vegetable stock
1 tbsp olive oil
2 slices pancetta or bacon, chopped
2 salmon fillets, skinned and sliced
  into strips
125ml double cream
1 tbsp chopped dill
squeeze of lemon juice
parsley leaves

Chicken and potato curried soup

1. Heat the oil in a frying pan. Add the chicken and fry until lightly browned. Remove from the pan and set aside.

2. Gently fry the onion until soft. Stir in the curry powder, cinnamon and garam masala. Cook for 1 minute and add the potatoes and carrots. Coat the vegetables in the oil and pour in the stock.

3. Bring to the boil and season with salt and pepper. Simmer gently until the vegetables are tender. Add the chicken and cook for 5 minutes or until it is cooked through.

4. Serve in warmed bowls garnished with the yoghurt and mint.

Preparation time: 10 min
Cooking time: 30 min
Serves 4

2 tbsp vegetable oil
2 chicken breasts, skinned and cut
   into cubes
1 onion, finely chopped
1 tbsp curry powder
½ tsp ground cinnamon
2 tsp garam masala
2 large potatoes, peeled and chopped
2 large carrots, peeled and chopped
750ml vegetable stock
4 tbsp yoghurt
mint leaves, roughly chopped

Pea soup

1. Heat the butter in a frying pan. Add the shallot and garlic and gently cook until softened.

2. Add the ginger, cook for 1 minute. Add the peas and stock and bring to a boil.

3. Simmer the soup for 6–8 minutes. Add the cream and blend to a smooth purée. Pass through a sieve and season to taste with salt and pepper.

4. Ladle the soup into bowls or beakers and add a swirl of crème fraîche to each.

Preparation time: 8 min
Cooking time: 12 min
Serves 4

2 tbsp butter
1 shallot, finely chopped
1 garlic clove, finely chopped
2cm piece fresh ginger, peeled and grated
400g frozen peas
600ml chicken stock
100ml double cream

2 tbsp crème fraîche, to serve

Wonton soup

Preparation time: 20 min
   plus 30 min
Cooking time: 20 min
Serves 4

For the wontons:
450g minced pork
thumb-size piece fresh ginger,
   peeled and grated
2 garlic cloves, finely chopped
2 tbsp rice vinegar
1 tbsp soy sauce
1 tbsp sesame oil
1 egg, whisked
32 wonton wrappers, thawed
   if frozen

For the broth:
1.2 litres chicken stock
2 tbsp soy sauce
2 tbsp rice vinegar
1 tbsp Sichuan pepper, crushed
4 spring onions (green parts only),
   finely sliced

1. Mix together all the ingredients for the wontons apart from the wrappers. Season with salt and pepper and set aside for 30 minutes.

2. Place a teaspoon of the wonton mixture in the middle of each wrapper. Moisten the edges with some water and gather up to make parcels, making sure they are well sealed.

3. Mix together the stock, soy sauce, rice vinegar and Sichuan pepper in a large pan. Bring to a boil and simmer for 10 minutes. Season with salt and pepper and drop in the wontons, a few at a time, and cook for about 3 minutes or until they have bobbed to the surface.

4. Remove the cooked wontons with a slotted spoon and place into warmed serving bowls. Pour over the broth and scatter with the spring onions.

71

Corn and crabmeat soup

1. Whisk together the egg white and sesame oil.

2. Bring the stock to the boil. Add the sweetcorn and simmer for about 4 minutes.

3. Add the rice wine, soy sauce, ginger, chilli, some salt and pepper and the sugar.

4. Mix the cornflour to a paste with 1 tablespoon cold water. Stir into the soup and bring to a boil.

5. Add the chopped crab. Slowly add the whisked egg white, stirring constantly, and season.

6. Ladle the soup into warmed bowls and serve scattered with the spring onions and coriander.

Preparation time: 10 min
Cooking time: 15 min
Serves 4

1 egg white
1 tsp sesame oil
1 litre chicken stock
400g tinned sweetcorn, drained
1 tbsp rice wine
1 tbsp light soy sauce
thumb-size piece fresh ginger, peeled and grated
1 red chilli, deseeded and finely chopped
1 tsp sugar
2 tsp cornflour
250g crabmeat, finely chopped
2 spring onions, finely chopped
1 tbsp chopped coriander leaves

Cold sorrel soup

1. Heat the butter in a large pan. Add the onion gently cook until soft but not brown.

2. Pour over the stock and bring to a boil. Add the sorrel and cook for 5 minutes or until the sorrel is tender.

3. Add the sugar and lemon juice, season with salt and pepper and add the cream. Chill for at least 2 hours.

Preparation time: 10 min
 plus 2 h chilling
Cooking time: 10 min
Serves 4

2 tbsp butter
1 onion, finely sliced
1 litre vegetable stock
450g sorrel, shredded
1 tbsp sugar
2 tbsp lemon juice
125ml double cream

Bean goulash

1. Heat the oil in a large pan. Add the onion, garlic and celery and fry until soft. Add the caraway, tomato purée and paprika and fry for a further 5 minutes.

2. Add the red wine and reduce the flame slightly. Add the stock and tomatoes and simmer gently for 20 minutes, stirring occasionally.

3. Pass the soup through a sieve. Return to the pan and gently reheat. Add the beans, peppers and red onion and season to taste with salt and cayenne pepper.

4. Rest for a few minutes to allow the flavours to mingle. Ladle into bowls and serve with a dollop of sour cream and a sprinkling of parsley and cayenne pepper.

Preparation time: 5 min
Cooking time: 30 min
Serves 4

2 tbsp olive oil
1 onion, finely chopped
2 garlic cloves, finely chopped
2 stalks celery, finely chopped
½ tsp caraway
1 tbsp tomato purée
1 tbsp spicy ground paprika
150ml red wine
600ml vegetable stock
400g tinned tomatoes, chopped
400g tinned kidney beans, rinsed and drained
2 red peppers, deseeded and finely chopped
1 red onion, finely chopped
cayenne pepper
4 tbsp sour cream
parsley sprigs

Clear broth with bacon dumplings and chives

Preparation time: 15 min
Cooking time: 20 min
Serves 4

1 tbsp butter
4 rashers smoked bacon, diced
1 onion, finely chopped
8 slices stale white bread,
    chopped into coarse breadcrumbs
4 tbsp chopped parsley
1 egg, whisked
125ml milk
1 tbsp flour
1 tsp dried marjoram
1.2 litres clear beef stock
chopped chives, to serve

1. Heat the butter in a frying pan. Add the bacon and gently fry until the fat starts to run. Add the onion and cook until it is soft but not brown.

2. Mix the onion and bacon with the breadcrumbs and parsley in a large bowl. Add the egg, milk, flour and marjoram. Season with salt and pepper and shape into 8 dumplings.

3. Heat the beef stock in a large pan until boiling. Add the dumplings and simmer gently for about 12 minutes.

4. Garnish with the chives.

Coconut and chicken soup

1. Heat the sesame oil in a wok. Add the chillies and lemongrass and cook for 2 minutes. Add the stock, coconut milk and lime leaves and simmer for about 10 minutes.

2. Add the chicken pieces to the soup and simmer gently until the chicken is cooked through. Add the fish sauce, lime juice and sugar, season with salt and pepper.

3. Serve in warmed bowls garnished with the coriander leaves.

Preparation time: 5 min
Cooking time: 15 min
Serves 4

2 tbsp sesame oil
2 red chillies, scored lengthways
2 stalks lemongrass, chopped
250ml coconut milk
750ml chicken stock
4 lime leaves
2 chicken breasts, skinned and cut
   into chunks
2 tbsp fish sauce
juice of 1 lime
1 tsp sugar
coriander leaves

Chestnut cream soup

1. Heat the oven to 425°F (220°C). Cut a cross on each chestnut with a sharp knife and place in a roasting tin. Bake in the oven for 15 minutes and let cool. Peel away the skins of the chestnuts.

2. Heat the butter in a large pan. Add the onion, celery, carrot and potato and gently fry until they have started to soften, and add the chestnuts.

3. Pour in the brandy. Let bubble and add the stock. Simmer for 20 minutes and add the cream and sugar. Simmer for 5 more minutes and season with salt and pepper.

4. Blend the soup until smooth and pass through a fine sieve into a clean pan. Reheat gently and serve with a dollop of crème fraîche sprinkled with chopped parsley.

Preparation time: 15 min
Cooking time: 45 min
Serves 4

450g fresh chestnuts
3 tbsp butter
1 onion, chopped
1 stalk celery, chopped
1 carrot, chopped
1 potato, chopped
100ml brandy
750ml vegetable stock
250ml double cream
pinch sugar
1 tablespoon chopped parsley
4 tbsp crème fraîche

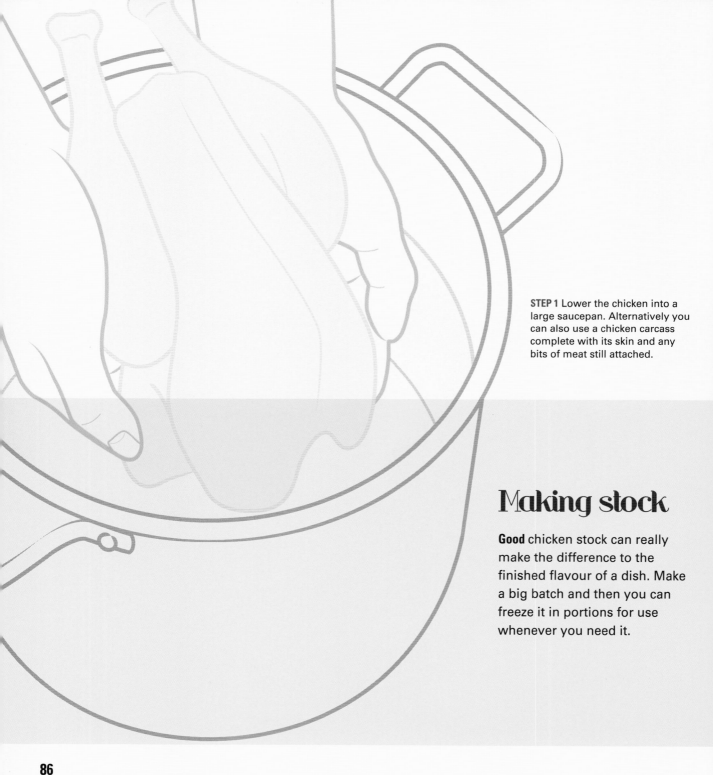

STEP 1 Lower the chicken into a large saucepan. Alternatively you can also use a chicken carcass complete with its skin and any bits of meat still attached.

Making stock

Good chicken stock can really make the difference to the finished flavour of a dish. Make a big batch and then you can freeze it in portions for use whenever you need it.

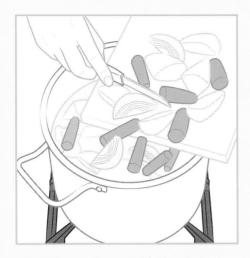

STEP 2 Chop up the vegetables into large chunks and tip them all into the saucepan with the chicken.

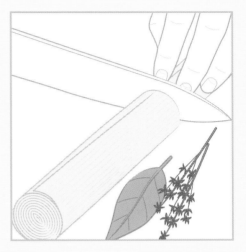

STEP 3 Trim the ends of a leek to make a tube shape. Remove the inner core of leaves.

STEP 4 Stuff the core of the leek with herbs and tie up with string to make a bouquet garni and drop into the stock.

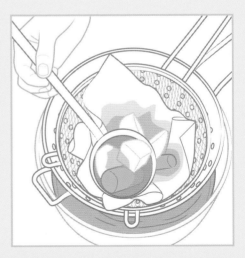

STEP 5 When the stock is ready, remove the chicken and strain through a sieve lined with kitchen paper.

Callaloo soup

1. Heat the oil in a large pan. Add the onion and garlic and gently cook until soft.

2. Add the okra and spinach. Cook for 2 minutes and add the water, bringing to a boil. Simmer gently for 30 minutes and add the parsley, prawns and thyme. Cook for another 10 minutes.

3. Blend to a smooth purée and pass through a fine sieve into a clean pan. Reheat gently and season with Tabasco, salt and pepper.

Preparation time: 20 min
Cooking time: 55 min
Serves 4

2 tbsp oil
1 onion, chopped
1 garlic clove, finely chopped
450g okra, sliced
450g spinach, washed
1 litre water
2 tbsp chopped parsley
200g prawns, peeled
1 teaspoon thyme, dried
Tabasco sauce, to taste

Cauliflower and roquefort soup

1. Place the vegetable stock into a pan and bring to the boil. Add the cauliflower and simmer gently for about 20 minutes or until the cauliflower is very tender.

2. While the soup is cooking, heat the oil in a frying pan. Add the bread and gently fry the cubes until golden brown. Drain on kitchen paper.

3. Blend the soup to a smooth purée, pass through a fine sieve into a clean pan and stir in the crème fraîche. Reheat gently and season with salt and pepper. Add nutmeg to taste.

4. Crumble the Roquefort into 4 bowls and ladle the hot soup over. Garnish with some freshly ground pepper, parsley and the croutons.

Preparation time: 10 min
Cooking time: 20 min
Serves 4

1 litre vegetable stock
600g cauliflower florets
2 tbsp olive oil
2 slices stale bread, cut into cubes
150ml crème fraîche
grated nutmeg
200g Roquefort cheese
1 tbsp finely chopped parsley

Kale and spinach soup

1. Heat the oil in a large pan. Add the onions, garlic and bacon and gently cook, stirring continually.

2. Add the carrot and potatoes and cook for 2 minutes. Add the wine and stock and simmer until the potatoes and carrots are soft.

3. Add the kale and spinach to the pan. Simmer for 5 more minutes and remove about a quarter of the vegetables. Set aside.

4. Blend the remaining mixture to a smooth purée. Return to the pan with the reserved vegetables and reheat gently. Season with the lemon juice, salt and pepper.

5. While the soup is cooking, heat the butter in a frying pan and gently fry the bread cubes until golden brown.

6. Serve the soup with the croutons and Parmesan on top and a dollop of crème fraîche.

Preparation time: 15 min
Cooking time: 35 min
Serves 4

2 tbsp vegetable oil
1 onion, chopped
1 garlic clove, chopped
2 rashers smoked bacon
1 carrot, diced
2 potatoes, diced
125ml white wine
800ml vegetable stock
300g kale, shredded
100g spinach, shredded
1 tsp lemon juice
2 tbsp butter
2 slices white bread, cut into cubes
4 tbsp grated Parmesan
2 tbsp crème fraîche

Cheese and leek soup

Preparation time: 5 min
Cooking time: 25 min
Serves 4

3 tbsp butter
450g leeks, finely sliced
2 tbsp flour
450ml chicken stock
250ml milk
100g soft blue cheese
1 tbsp finely chopped dill
croutons

1. Melt the butter in a pan. Add the leeks and gently cook for about 5 minutes.

2. Sprinkle over the flour and cook for a further 2–3 minutes. Gradually add the stock and the milk. Stir well, then cover and simmer over a low heat for about 15 minutes.

3. Dice the cheese, add to the soup and let it melt slowly. Season the soup with the dill, salt and pepper. Ladle into warmed bowls and scattered with croutons.

Alsatian sausage and lentil soup

1. Heat the vegetable oil in a large pan. Add the bacon and gently cook until the fat runs. Add the onion and leek and cook until soft. Add the garlic, carrots and potatoes and cook for 2 minutes.

2. Add the cloves, bay leaf and stock. Bring to a boil and add the lentils. Simmer for 30–40 minutes or until the lentils are soft. Season with salt and pepper.

3. Peel the skin off the sausage, slice it and it add to the soup. Heat through and serve in warmed bowls with some parsley scattered over.

Preparation time: 15 min
  plus overnight soaking
Cooking time: 50 min
Serves 4

2 tbsp vegetable oil
100g cubed bacon
1 onion, chopped
1 leek, finely sliced
1 garlic clove, finely chopped
2 carrots, finely chopped
2 medium potatoes, finely diced
2 cloves
1 bay leaf
1.5 litres beef stock
150g brown lentils, soaked overnight
250g mortadella sausage
2 tbsp chopped parsley

Chilli tomato soup with prawns

1. Heat the olive oil. Add the onion and gently cook until soft but not brown. Add the garlic, cook for 1 more minute then add the paprika and chilli.

2. Stir for 1 minute then add the pepper, tomatoes, tomato purée, stock and sugar. Bring to the boil and simmer very gently for 30 minutes.

3. Season with salt and pepper, blend to a smooth purée then pass through a fine sieve into a clean pan.

4. Reheat gently then pour into warmed bowls and serve with the crème fraîche, prawns and chilli flakes on top and some pesto on the side.

Preparation time: 10 min
Cooking time: 35 min
Serves 4

2 tbsp olive oil
1 onion, chopped
1 garlic clove, chopped
2 tsp sweet paprika
1 red chilli, deseeded and chopped
1 red pepper, deseeded and chopped
400g tinned tomatoes, chopped
4 tbsp tomato purée
750ml vegetable stock
½ tsp sugar
4 tbsp crème fraîche
8–12 cooked prawns, skewered onto cocktail sticks
1 good pinch chilli flakes
Spinach pesto

Asian-style vegetable noodle soup

1. Place the stock into a pan with the crushed lemongrass and chopped ginger and bring to a boil. Simmer for 5 minutes and strain through a sieve into a clean pan.

2. Cook the noodles according to the pack instructions, refresh in cold water and drain.

3. Return the stock to the boil, and add the garlic, mushrooms, carrot, spring onions and chilli. Simmer gently for 2–3 minutes and add the soy sauce, fish sauce and sugar.

4. Add the noodles and sesame oil. Heat through gently and serve with the parsley scattered over.

Preparation time: 15 min
Cooking time: 15 min
Serves 4

800ml chicken stock
4 stalks lemongrass, crushed
thumb-size piece fresh ginger, peeled and chopped
100g Chinese egg noodles
1 garlic clove, finely chopped
100g button mushrooms, finely sliced
1 carrot, finely sliced
4 spring onions, sliced
1 red chilli, deseeded and finely sliced
2 tbsp soy sauce
1 tbsp fish sauce
1 tsp sugar
1 tsp sesame oil
2 tbsp parsley, roughly chopped

Green potato and celeriac leaf soup

Preparation time: 10 min
Cooking time: 35 min
Serves 4

*4 medium potatoes, peeled and
    chopped*
2 garlic cloves, chopped
2 spring onions, chopped
1 bunch celeriac leaves
1 litre vegetable stock
4 tbsp crème fraîche
2 tbsp double cream
pinch of grated nutmeg
*2 slices bacon, halved and fried
    until crisp*

1. Place the potatoes, garlic and spring onions in a large pan. Reserving a few celeriac leaves to garnish, roughly chop the remainder and add to the pan.

2. Pour over the stock. Bring to a boil and simmer gently until the potatoes are soft. Season with salt and pepper and blend to a smooth purée.

3. Stir in the crème fraîche and cream. Reheat gently and add nutmeg to taste.

4. Serve the soup in warm bowls with the reserved celeriac leaves and the bacon.

Bortsch

1. Heat the oil in a large pan. Add the onion and garlic and gently cook until soft but not browned.

2. Add the celery, beetroot and cabbage and cook for 5 minutes, stirring from time to time.

3. Add the stock, bring to a boil and simmer for 15–20 minutes. Add the lemon juice and chopped dill and season with salt and pepper.

4. Serve in warmed bowls with a dollop of sour cream and a dill sprig.

Preparation time: 10 min
Cooking time: 30 min
Serves 4

2 tbsp oil
2 onions, finely chopped
2 garlic cloves
1 stalk celery, chopped
600g beetroot, peeled and finely diced
200g white cabbage, finely chopped
1.5 litres vegetable or chicken stock
juice of ½ lemon
4 tbsp sour cream
1 tbsp chopped dill sprigs

Cep and mushroom soup with cured, smoked pork loin

1. Heat about 150ml of the stock in a small pan. Add the ceps and remove from the heat. Set aside to soak for 30 minutes.

2. Heat the oil in a large pan. Add the onions and garlic and gently cook until soft. Add the button mushrooms and cook very gently, stirring from time to time, for 5 minutes.

3. Strain the ceps through a fine sieve, reserving the stock, and add the ceps to the pan. Add the cep stock and the remaining vegetable stock. Season with salt and pepper, bring to a boil and simmer gently for 15–20 minutes.

4. Meanwhile, heat some more oil in a small pan. Add the pork and quickly cook until golden brown.

5. Remove a few mushroom and ceps from the soup and set aside. Blend the remainder to a very smooth purée. Add the crème fraîche, reheat gently and pour into warmed bowls.

6. Garnish with a swirl of cream, the chopped parsley and reserved mushrooms, ceps and pork cubes.

Preparation time: 15 min
  plus 30 min soaking
Cooking time: 45 min
Serves 4

750ml vegetable stock
25g dried ceps, washed
2 tbsp vegetable oil
2 red onions, finely choppped
1 garlic clove, chopped
200g button mushrooms, sliced
150g smoked loin of pork, finely
  diced
2 tbsp crème fraîche
2 tbsp double cream
chopped parsley

Nettle soup

1. Heat the butter in a pan. Add the onions and potato and cook until soft but not brown.

2. Add the stock and cook for about 25 minutes, until the vegetables are very soft.

3. Chop the nettles and add to the soup. Cook briefly and blend to a smooth purée. Pass through a fine sieve into a clean pan. Season with salt and pepper and add lemon juice and nutmeg to taste.

4. Reheat gently then stir in the cream. Ladle the soup into soup plates and garnish each with a spoonful of crème fraîche and a few chives.

Preparation time: 10 min
Cooking time: 35 min
Serves 4

2 tbsp butter
1 onion, finely chopped
3 medium potatoes, peeled and
    finely diced
750ml vegetable stock
450g young nettle leaves, washed
1 tsp lemon juice
pinch of grated nutmeg
100ml double cream
4 tbsp crème fraîche
snipped chives

Herb soup

1. Blanch the spinach in boiling, salted water until it has wilted. Refresh in cold water, drain well and chop.

2. Heat the butter in a large pan. Add the shallot and gently cook until soft. Add the potatoes and pour in the stock. Bring to the boil and simmer for about 10 minutes.

3. Reserve a few herbs and add the remainder to the pan with the spinach and cream. Bring to a boil and purée until smooth.

4. Cut the crusts off the bread and chop into cubes. Heat the olive oil and fry the bread until golden brown.

5. Reheat the soup gently. Season with salt and pepper and serve in warmed bowls with the croutons and reserved herbs on top.

Preparation time: 15 min
Cooking time: 25 min
Serves 4

2 handfuls spinach, washed
2 tbsp butter
1 shallot, finely chopped
2 medium potatoes, peeled and
    grated
750ml chicken stock
2 handfuls mixed soft herbs, eg
    chervil, parsley, basil, sorrel,
    tarragon
175ml double cream
2 slices white bread
2 tbsp olive oil

Gazpacho

1. Soak the bread in cold water for 5 minutes. Squeeze out the water and put the bread in a food processor or blender.

2. Add the tomatoes, garlic, oil, vinegar and sugar and blend to a smooth purée. Add some cold water, if needed, and pass through a fine sieve into a bowl. Season with salt and pepper and chill for at least 2 hours.

3. Garnish with the cucumber and egg.

Preparation time: 15 min
  plus 2 h chilling
Serves 4

4 slices stale white bread
12 large very ripe tomatoes
2 garlic cloves, chopped
2 tbsp olive oil
1 tbsp red wine vinegar
pinch of sugar
½ cucumber, finely chopped
2 hard-boiled eggs, finely chopped

Scotch broth

Preparation time: 20 min
Cooking time: 2 h 15 min
Serves 6

2 tbsp butter
1 tbsp oil
1 onion, chopped
450g lamb breast, diced
1 small swede, diced
2 large carrots, roughly chopped
1 large potato, peeled and diced
50g pearl barley
1.5 litres lamb stock
1 leek, thinly sliced
1 stalk celery, sliced

1. Heat the butter and oil in a pan. Add the onion and lamb and cook over a high heat until browned.

2. Add the rest of the ingredients, except the leek and celery, to the pan and bring to a boil.

3. Turning the heat down, cover and cook very gently for 1 hour. Add the leeks and celery and cook for another hour until the meat is very tender.

4. Season with salt and pepper.

Spicy beef soup

1. Cook the pasta in boiling, salted water according to the pack instructions until tender and crisp. Rinse under cold water, then drain.

2. Bring the stock to a boil with the lemongrass and lime leaves. Add the carrots, peppers, beans and chilli peppers and simmer for about 5 minutes.

3. Add the beef, spring onions and pasta. Season with chilli sauce, fish sauce, sugar and lime juice and simmer until the beef is just cooked through.

4. Pour into warmed bowls.

Preparation time: 10 min
Cooking time: 15 min
Serves 4

100g ribbon pasta
800ml beef stock
1 stalk lemongrass, slightly crushed
   and chopped
2 lime leaves
2 carrots, sliced into half moons
2 red peppers, deseeded and cut
   into strips
200g string beans, sliced
2 green chilli peppers, finely
   chopped
300g beef, finely sliced
1 bunch spring onions, sliced
hot chilli sauce, to taste
fish sauce, to taste
1 tsp sugar
juice of 1 lime

Thai soup with fried salmon skewers

1. Mix the salmon with the sesame oil and set aside. Set 4 stalks of lemongrass aside and finely chop the remaining one.

2. Place the chilli, ginger, chopped lemongrass, spring onions and coconut milk in a large pan with about 250ml water.

3. Bring to a boil and simmer for 10 minutes. Add the fish sauce, lime juice and sugar and continue cooking very gently.

4. Thread the salmon cubes onto the remaining 4 stalks of lemongrass. Fry in a hot pan for about 2 minutes on each side, turning frequently, or until the fish is cooked through.

5. Season the soup with salt and pepper, add the chard and peanuts and ladle into warmed bowls. Serve with the salmon skewers.

Preparation time: 15 min
Cooking time: 15 min
Serves 4

450g salmon fillet, cut into cubes
2 tbsp sesame oil
5 stalks lemongrass
1 red chilli, deseeded and finely chopped
thumb-size piece fresh ginger, peeled and finely chopped
2 spring onions, finely chopped
750ml coconut milk
2 tbsp fish sauce
juice of 1 lime
1 tsp sugar
2 large chard leaves, roughly shredded
2 tbsp chopped peanuts

Broccoli, sweetcorn and mushroom soup

1. Heat the oil in a pan. Add the onion and garlic and cook until soft but not brown.

2. Add the mushrooms. Cook very gently for 5 minutes and add the stock. Bring to a boil. Add the broccoli and simmer for 10 minutes. Add the sweetcorn.

3. Mix the flour and butter together to form a paste. Stir it into the soup with the cream and simmer for 2 minutes.

4. Season with salt and pepper and stir in the parsley.

Preparation time: 10 min
Cooking time: 30 min
Serves 4

2 tbsp vegetable oil
1 onion, finely chopped
2 garlic cloves, finely chopped
200g chopped button mushrooms
800ml vegetable stock
350g broccoli florets
1 small can sweetcorn, drained and rinsed
1 tbsp flour
2 tbsp butter
125ml double cream
1 tbsp chopped parsley

Cream of celeriac soup

Preparation time: 10 min
Cooking time: 30 min
Serves 4

2 tbsp butter
1 onion, finely chopped
1 potato, chopped
450g celeriac, peeled and chopped
750ml vegetable stock
75g blue cheese
250ml double cream
celery leaves or parsley

1. Heat the butter in a large pan. Add the onion and gently cook until soft but not brown.

2. Add the potato and celeriac, cook for 2 minutes and add the stock. Bring to a boil then simmer gently for 20 minutes or until the vegetables are very soft. Stir in the cheese until it has melted.

3. Reserve some cream to garnish and add the rest to the soup. Blend to a smooth purée and pass through a fine sieve into a clean pan. Reheat gently, season with salt and pepper and serve with a swirl of cream and the celery leaves or parsley.

Apricot soup

1. Place the apricots and their juice in a blender or food processor with the apricot nectar and liqueur and blend until you have a smooth purée.

2. Pass through a fine sieve and chill for at least 1 hour.

3. Mix the raspberries with the lemon juice and sugar and pass through a fine sieve.

4. Serve the chilled soup with a swirl of the raspberry coulis and garnish with a mint sprig.

Preparation time: 15 min
   plus 1 h chilling
Serves 4

800g tinned apricots
50ml apricot nectar
1 tsp apricot liqueur
100g raspberries, defrosted if
   frozen
1 tbsp lemon juice
1 tbsp sugar
sprigs mint

Haddock soup

1. Heat the butter in a large pan. Add the onion and gently cook until soft but not brown.

2. Stir in the paprika, chopped peppers, chilli pepper and potatoes and cook for 2 minutes, stirring all the time.

3. Pour in the wine and stock. Bring to a boil and simmer gently until the potatoes are tender.

4. Add the haddock and sweetcorn to the pan and simmer for 5 minutes. Stir in the crème fraîche and parsley and season with salt and pepper.

Preparation time: 10 min
Cooking time: 30 min
Serves 4

2 tbsp butter
1 onion, finely sliced
1 tsp paprika
1 red pepper, deseeded and
   finely chopped
1 green pepper, deseeded and
   finely chopped
1 red chilli pepper, deseeded and
   finely chopped
2 medium potatoes, peeled and
   finely diced
125ml white wine
150ml fish stock
2 smoked haddock fillets, cut
   into chunks
140g tinned sweetcorn, drained
125ml crème fraîche
2 tbsp chopped parsley

Making wontons

A good broth can be a delicious and healthy lunch, but with the addition of freshly made wontons it can become a hearty and filling meal. They look impressive but are oh so easy to make.

STEP 1 Mix together all the filling ingredients for the wontons in a large bowl. It's easiest to do this with your fingers.

STEP 2 Lay a wonton wrapper flat on a work surface and place a teaspoonful of filling mixture in the middle of the wrapper.

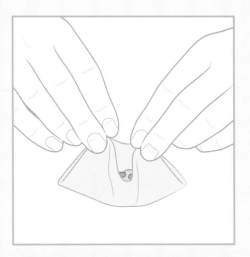

STEP 3 Moisten the edges of the wonton wrapper with a little water and gather them up around the filling to make parcels, pinching to seal well.

STEP 4 For added security, tie the wontons around the neck of the parcels using a spring onion strand.

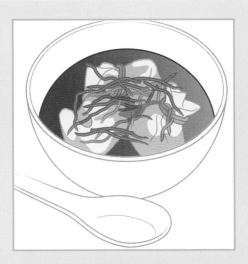

STEP 5 Bring the broth to the boil and lower in the wontons. Cook for 3 minutes or until they rise to the surface.

Creamed sweetcorn soup with fried bacon

1. Heat the butter in a large pan. Add the onion and gently cook until soft. Reserve some of the chopped chilli for the garnish and add the rest to the pan.

2. Sprinkle the flour into the pan. Cook for 1 minute, stirring all the time, then gradually add the stock.

3. Bring to a boil and simmer gently for 10 minutes. Reserve about a quarter of the sweetcorn and add the remainder to the pan. Blend until smooth and pass through a fine sieve into a clean pan.

4. Stir in the cream and the remaining sweetcorn. Reheat gently and season with salt and pepper. Garnish with the remaining red chilli, the crumbled bacon and the parsley.

Preparation time: 10 min
Cooking time: 20 min
Serves 4

2 tbsp butter
1 onion, finely chopped
1 red chilli, deseeded and
   finely chopped
2 tbsp flour
750ml vegetable stock
280g tinned sweetcorn, drained
125ml double cream
2 rashers bacon, fried until crisp
   and crumbled
sprigs parsley

White bean and sausage soup

1. Heat the oil in a large pan. Add the onion and celery and gently cook until soft.

2. Add the garlic and carrots and cook for 2 minutes. Add the stock. Bring to a boil and add the sausages. Simmer for 15 minutes.

3. Add the beans. Season with salt and pepper and add the parsley. Simmer for 5 more minutes.

Preparation time: 10 min
Cooking time: 25 min
Serves 4

3 tbsp olive oil
1 onion, finely chopped
2 stalks celery, finely chopped
2 garlic cloves, finely chopped
2 carrots, finely chopped
750ml chicken or vegetable stock
2 large pork sausages, sliced
400g tinned haricot beans, drained and rinsed
4 tbsp chopped parsley

Californian salmon soup

1. Pour the water into a large pan. Add the celery, leek, shallots, ginger and bay leaf. Bring to a boil. Add the tomatoes, cinnamon and nutmeg. Simmer gently for 30 minutes.

2. Blend to a smooth purée. Pass through a fine sieve into a clean pan.

3. Add the cream and simmer for 4 minutes. Add the salmon and continue cooking for 3–4 minutes or until the salmon is just cooked through.

4. Add the lime juice and chives. Season with salt and pepper and pour into warmed bowls. Garnish with the dill sprigs.

Preparation time: 10 min
Cooking time: 40 min
Serves 4

750ml water
1 stalk celery, chopped
1 leek, chopped
2 shallots, chopped
thumb-size piece fresh ginger
1 bay leaf
200g tinned tomatoes, chopped
pinch ground cinnamon
pinch grated nutmeg
125ml double cream
350g salmon fillet, cut into chunks
juice of 1 lime
2 tbsp chopped chives
dill sprigs, to serve

Salmon and asparagus red curry soup

Preparation time: 10 min
Cooking time: 35 min
Serves 4

4 tbsp vegetable oil
1 garlic clove, finely sliced
2 chilli peppers, deseeded
    and sliced
1 stalk lemongrass, crushed and
    chopped
thumb-sized piece ginger, peeled
    and sliced
2 tbsp red curry paste
400ml coconut milk
600ml fish stock
12 spears white asparagus
12 spears green asparagus
450g salmon fillet, cut into chunks
light soy sauce
coriander leaves

1. Heat 2 tablespoons of the oil in a large pan. Add the garlic, chilli, lemongrass and ginger and gently cook for about 3 minutes.

2. Stir in the curry paste and pour in the coconut milk and fish stock. Gently simmer for 20 minutes.

3. Peel the white asparagus and the lower third of the green asparagus. Steam the white asparagus over salted, boiling water for 5 minutes. Add the green asparagus and cook for a further 5 minutes until nearly tender. Allow to cool slightly and chop diagonally into pieces.

4. Heat the remaining oil in a frying pan. Cook the salmon for 30 seconds on each side and season with salt.

5. Place the salmon and asparagus in the soup. Season with the soy sauce and heat through. Garnish with coriander.

Curried parsnip soup

1. Heat the butter in a large pan. Add the onion and cook until soft but not brown.

2. Add the parsnips and potato and stir in the curry powder. Cook for 2 minutes.

3. Stir in the stock and simmer gently, stirring occasionally, for about 30 minutes.

4. Add the cream and blend the soup to a smooth purée. Pass through a fine sieve into a clean pan. Reheat gently and season to taste with salt and pepper.

5. Pour into warmed bowls. Garnish with cayenne pepper and sesame seeds and sprinkle with chopped coriander leaves.

Preparation time: 10 min
Cooking time: 40 min
Serves 4

2 tbsp butter
1 onion, chopped
600g parsnips, peeled and chopped
1 large potato, peeled and chopped
2–3 tsp mild curry powder
1 litre vegetable stock
125ml double cream
cayenne pepper
1 tbsp toasted sesame seeds
fresh coriander leaves

Lamb and cabbage soup

1. Heat the oil in a large pan. Add the meat and brown on all sides.

2. Add the bacon, onion, garlic and chilli powder and cook for 5 minutes, stirring from time to time. Add the stock.

3. Bring to a boil. Add the potatoes, pumpkin and carrot. Simmer for 40 minutes.

4. Season with salt and pepper. Add the cabbage and cauliflower and cook for a further 15 minutes.

5. Stir in the chopped dill.

Preparation time: 10 min
Cooking time: 1 h
Serves 4

2 tbsp olive oil
450g lamb leg, cut into large chunks
4 rashers bacon, chopped
1 onion, chopped
1 garlic clove, chopped
1 tsp chilli powder
1 litre lamb stock
2 medium potatoes, chopped
200g pumpkin or squash, peeled
  and chopped
1 carrot, chopped
½ small cabbage, shredded
200g cauliflower florets
2 tbsp chopped dill

Coconut, chicken and vegetable soup

1. Heat the oil in a wok. Add the vegetables and chilli and briefly toss in the hot oil.

2. Add the stock and simmer for about 10 minutes. Add the chicken and cook gently for a further 10 minutes.

3. Add the coconut milk. Heat gently and season with salt and pepper. Pull the chicken apart with a fork. Ladle into warmed soup bowls and garnish with the coriander.

Preparation time: 10 min
Cooking time: 25 min
Serves 4

2 tbsp sesame oil
3 carrots, peeled and finely sliced
1 stalk lemongrass, sliced
2 spring onions, sliced
1 onion, finely sliced
1 red chilli, deseeded and sliced
750ml chicken stock
2 chicken breasts, skinned
200ml coconut milk
coriander leaves

Red lentil, ginger, fennel and chilli soup

Preparation time: 10 min
Cooking time: 35 min
Serves 4

2 tbsp oil
1 red onion, finely chopped
1 bulb fennel, finely chopped
2 red chilli peppers, deseeded and
  finely sliced
thumb-sized piece fresh ginger,
  peeled and grated
2 tsp curry powder
200g red lentils, rinsed and
  drained
1 litre chicken stock
1 spring onion, green parts only

1. Heat the oil in a large pan. Add the onion, fennel and chilli and cook until softened. Add the ginger and curry powder and cook for 2 more minutes.

2. Stir in the lentils and pour in the stock. Bring to a boil. Cover and simmer over a low heat for 20–30 minutes, until the lentils are soft.

3. Season with salt and pepper. Ladle into warmed bowls and garnish with the spring onion leaves.

Lobster minestrone

1. Heat the oil in a large pan. Add the leek, carrot and celery and gently cook for 5 minutes.

2. Add the stock and bring to a boil. Add the pasta shells and cook until nearly tender, adding the cabbage for the last few minutes.

3. Meanwhile, remove the meat from the body and the claws of the lobster and chop into chunks. Place the lobster meat in the pan and heat through gently.

4. Add the lemon juice. Season with salt and pepper and garnish with the tarragon.

Preparation time: 15 min
Cooking time: 25 min
Serves 4

2 tbsp olive oil
1 leek, finely chopped
1 carrot, finely diced
1 stalk celery, finely diced
1 litre fish or shellfish stock
150g pasta shells
¼ Savoy cabbage, shredded
1 large cooked lobster
juice of 1 lemon
tarragon sprigs

Cold melon soup with prawns

1. Place the melon, 1 garlic clove, the yoghurt and sherry into a food processor or blender. Blend to a smooth purée. Season to taste and chill for at least 2 hours.

2. Heat the oil in a wide pan and briefly cook the tomatoes until they start to soften. Remove from the pan, sprinkle with some salt and set aside.

3. Heat the pan and add the prawns and cayenne pepper. Cook on a high heat for 2–3 minutes or until the prawns are cooked through, stirring all the time. Once cooked, thread the prawns onto cocktail sticks.

4. Pour the chilled soup into serving glasses. Add the tomatoes and marjoram and top with a prawn skewer.

Preparation time:
  plus 2 h chilling
Cooking time: 20 min
Serves 4

1 Galia melon, seeds removed and
  flesh chopped
2 garlic cloves
4 tbsp yoghurt
3 tbsp dry sherry
2 tbsp olive oil
4 red cherry tomatoes, halved
4 yellow cherry tomatoes, halved
8 large prawns, shelled
pinch cayenne pepper
fresh marjoram

Spicy split pea and chicken soup

1. Heat the oil in a large pan. Add the onion and celery and gently cook until soft.

2. Stir in the curry powder and cumin. Cook for 1 minute and add the carrot and chillies. Add the split peas and the stock. Season with salt and pepper and simmer gently for 30 minutes.

3. Add the chicken and continue cooking until the spilt peas are very soft and the chicken is cooked through.

4. Reserve about a quarter of the soup and blend the remaining to a purée. Return to the pan with the reserved soup. Reheat gently and pour into warmed bowls.

5. Garnish with the spring onions, chopped cashew nuts and coriander leaves scattered over.

Preparation time: 5 min
Cooking time: 40 min
Serves 4

3 tbsp vegetable oil
1 onion, finely chopped
1 stalk celery, finely chopped
1 tbsp curry powder
1 tsp ground cumin
1 carrot, finely chopped
2 red chillies, deseeded and
   finely sliced
200g split peas
750ml chicken stock
2 chicken breasts, skinned and cubed
2 spring onions, sliced, to serve
2 tbsp chopped cashew nuts, to serve
coriander leaves, to serve

Chicken and sweetcorn soup

1. Heat the butter in a large pan. Add the onion and gently cook until soft. Add the garlic, curry powder and turmeric, cook for 2 minutes and add the potatoes.

2. Cook for 2 more minutes and add the sweetcorn and stock. Bring to a boil. Season with salt and pepper and simmer gently until the potatoes are tender.

3. Add the diced chicken, cook for 10 more minutes and stir in the cream and tomato. Mash the vegetables slightly with a fork or potato masher. Check the seasoning and add Tabasco to taste.

4. Serve in warmed bowls with the grilled bread.

Preparation time: 10 min
Cooking time: 35 min
Serves 4

2 tbsp butter
1 onion, finely chopped
1 garlic clove, finely chopped
2 tsp curry powder
1 tsp turmeric
2 medium potatoes, peeled and finely diced
280g tinned sweetcorn, drained
500ml vegetable stock
2 chicken breasts, skinned and diced
250ml double cream
1 tomato, peeled, deseeded and chopped
tabasco sauce
4 slices grilled French bread

Creamed spinach soup

1. Heat the oil. Add the onion and cook the onion until soft. Add the potato and cook, stirring, for 2 minutes.

2. Add the stock and bring to the boil. Cook gently until the potato is tender. Add the spinach and cook until wilted.

3. Meanwhile heat the butter in a small pan. Add the shallot and cook until brown and crisp. Drain on kitchen paper.

4. When the soup is cooked, purée with a hand blender. Add the cream and gently reheat. Season with salt and pepper.

5. Ladle the soup into bowls and garnish with the fried shallot.

Preparation time: 5 min
Cooking time: 20 min
Serves 4

2 tbsp vegetable oil
1 onion, chopped
1 large potato, chopped
750ml vegetable stock
900g spinach, stalks discarded
2 tbsp butter
1 shallot, finely sliced
250ml double cream

Tomato and beetroot soup with feta cheese

Preparation time: 5 min
plus 2 h chilling if
serving cold
Cooking time: 30 min
Serves 4

2 tbsp oil
1 onion, chopped
1 garlic clove, chopped
450g beetroot, peeled
  and chopped
750ml vegetable stock
200g tinned tomatoes, chopped
juice of 1 lemon
100g feta cheese, diced
fresh oregano

1. Heat the oil in a large pan. Add the onions and garlic and cook until soft but not brown.

2. Add the beetroot, cook for 5 minutes and add the stock and tomatoes. Bring to a boil and simmer for 15–20 minutes or until the beetroot is tender.

3. Blend to a smooth purée and season with the lemon juice, salt and pepper. Either chill for at least 2 hours before serving or serve hot.

4. Pour the soup into bowl, sprinkle over the feta cheese and garnish with the oregano.

Creamy pumpkin soup

1. Heat the butter and oil in a large pan and cook the onion and garlic until soft but not brown.

2. Add the pumpkin, potatoes and carrot. Cook for 2 minutes, stirring all the time. Add the stock.

3. Bring to a boil and simmer gently for 20–25 minutes or until the vegetables are very tender.

4. Blend to a smooth purée then pass through a fine sieve into a clean pan. Reheat gently and season with salt and pepper.

5. Serve the soup in warmed bowls garnished with a swirl of yoghurt and thyme leaves.

Preparation time: 10 min
Cooking time: 35 min
Serves 4

2 tbsp butter
1 tbsp oil
1 onion, chopped
1 garlic clove, chopped
1 medium pumpkin, peeled, deseeded and diced
2 medium potatoes, peeled and chopped
1 carrot, peeled and chopped
1 litre chicken stock
4 tbsp yoghurt, to serve
3 sprigs thyme, leaves only, to serve

Watercress soup with salmon and herbs

1. Place the salmon fillets in a pan with the wine and enough water to cover. Bring to a boil and simmer gently for 3–4 minutes or until the salmon is just cooked through. Remove the salmon from the pan and set aside in a warm place. Return the pan to the heat and boil until the liquid has reduced by two-thirds.

2. Heat the butter in a clean panand add the shallots and garlic. Cook until soft but not brown. Add the potatoes and cook for 2 minutes.

3. Add the stock, bring to a boil and simmer gently until the potatoes are tender. Add the watercress, cook for 3 minutes then stir in the herbs and the cream.

4. Purée until smooth and return to the pan. Season with salt and pepper and reheat gently.

5. Toast the bread on both sides. Pour the soup into warmed bowls, divide the fish between the bowls and serve with the toasted bread.

Preparation time: 10 min
Cooking time: 30 min
Serves 4

2 salmon fillets
125ml white wine
2 tbsp butter
2 shallots, chopped
1 garlic clove, chopped
2 medium potatoes, peeled and diced
750ml vegetable stock
1 bunch watercress, washed
2 tbsp chopped mixed herbs, dill,
*   parsley, chervil, chives, etc.*
125ml double cream
8 slices French bread

Italian fish soup

1. Wash the mussels, remove the beards and discard any that do not open when tapped. Set aside.

2. Drop the tomatoes in boiling water, leave for 30 seconds and drain. Peel off the skins, remove the seeds and chop the flesh.

3. Heat the oil in a large pan. Add and cook the onion and celery until soft. Add the garlic and chilli, cook for 1 minute, then add the potatoes and tomatoes and cook for 2 more minutes.

4. Pour in the wine and stock, bring to a boil and season with salt and pepper. Simmer gently for 20 minutes or until the potatoes are tender.

5. Add the white fish, simmer for 2 minutes and add the prawns and mussels. Cook until the mussels have opened. Check the seasoning and stir in the parsley. Discard any mussels that remain closed.

Preparation time: 15 min
Cooking time: 40 min
Serves 4

450g mussels
2 medium tomatoes
4 tbsp olive oil
1 onion, finely chopped
1 stalk celery, finely chopped
2 garlic cloves, finely chopped
1 red chilli pepper, deseeded
  and chopped
2 medium potatoes, peeled
  and chopped
125ml white wine
500ml fish stock or water
450g white fish fillet, cut into chunks
250g prawns, shell on
3 tbsp chopped parsley

Spicy sweet potato and ginger soup

Preparation time: 10 min
Cooking time: 25 min
Serves 4

2 tbsp oil
2 onions, chopped
1 garlic clove, chopped
1 thumb-sized piece fresh ginger,
    peeled and grated
1 red chilli, deseeded and chopped
2 sweet potatoes, peeled and
    cubed
2 tbsp sherry vinegar
1 litre vegetable stock
100ml sour cream
 pinch of ground cinnamon
75g goat's cheese
zest of 1 lime

1. Heat the oil in a saucepan and add the onions. Cook until soft. Add the garlic, ginger and chilli and cook for 2 minutes.

2. Add the sweet potatoes, stir for 2 minutes and add the vinegar and the stock. Cover with a lid and simmer for about 15 minutes until the potatoes are soft.

3. Purée the soup with a hand blender, stir in the sour cream and gently reheat. Season with salt, pepper and cinnamon.

4. Ladle the soup into bowls and crumble over some goat's cheese and lime zest.

Fish soup

1. Heat the butter in a frying pan and add the bread cubes. Gently fry until golden brown. Drain on kitchen paper and set aside.

2. Drop the tomatoes in boiling water, leave for 30 seconds and drain. Peel off the skin, remove the seeds and chop the flesh.

3. Place the stock and wine or vermouth in a large pan, bring to a boil and add the leek, carrots, thyme and tomatoes. Simmer for 5 minutes.

4. Add the fish and prawns. Season with salt and pepper and simmer until the the fish is just cooked through.

5. Serve the soup with the croutons scattered over.

Preparation time: 20 min
Cooking time: 20 min
Serves 4

2 tbsp butter
2 slices stale white bread, diced
2 tomatoes
1 litre fish stock
125ml white wine or vermouth
1 leek, sliced
2 carrots, cut into fine strands
2 tbsp thyme leaves
450g fish fillets, cut into chunks
250g prawns, shelled

Carrot and tomato soup

1. Heat the oil in a large pan and gently add the onion and celery. Cook until soft.

2. Stir in the garlic, carrots and tomatoes and add the stock or water.

3. Bring to a boil and simmer for 15–20 minutes or until the carrots are tender.

4. Blend until smooth and pass through a fine sieve into a clean pan. Add a little more water if needed. Season with salt and freshly ground pepper and reheat gently. Serve in warmed bowls garnished with ground pink peppercorns, if you like.

Preparation time: 5 min
Cooking time: 25 min
Serves 4

2 tbsp olive oil
1 onion, finely chopped
1 stalk celery, finely chopped
1 garlic clove, chopped
4 large carrots, peeled and chopped
450g tomatoes, chopped
750ml vegetable stock or water
freshly ground pink peppercorns
  (optional), to serve

STEP 1 If you have an electric blender, pour the cooked soup into the jug. You may need to do this in batches.

Pureeing soups

How smooth or chunky you like your soup depends on your personal preference, but many soup recipes call for blending or pureeing for a smoother texture.

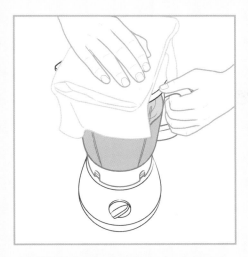

STEP 2 Put the lid on and cover an open top with a towel to protect yourself against the hot liquid. Blend until it reaches your preferred consistency.

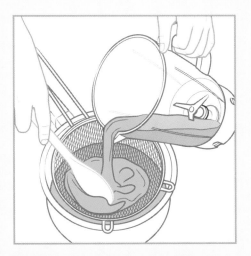

STEP 3 If you want a really smooth finish to your soup, pour the blended soup into a sieve set over a bowl. Push the soup through into the bowl.

STEP 4 You can also use a stick blender. Simply submerge it and circle it round the pan until evenly blended.

STEP 5 Pour the blended soup into a clean pan and reheat gently. Serve in bowls with a swirl of cream.

Mushroom, chicken and watercress soup

1. Heat the oil in a large pan and add the chicken. Fry for 5 minutes or until golden brown all over. Remove from the pan and set aside.

2. Add the onion, garlic and celery to the pan and cook for 5 minutes.

3. Add the chopped mushrooms, thyme and sherry. Season to taste and cook the vegetables for 2–3 minutes, stirring occasionally. Reserve some mushrooms for the garnish.

4. Transfer the mixture to a food processor or blender and add half the stock. Process until smooth and return to the pan. Add the remaining stock. Return the chicken to the pan and heat until boiling. Simmer for 3 minutes. Stir in the cream and heat through.

5. Ladle into bowls or mugs and top with the reserved mushrooms and the watercress.

Preparation time: 10 min
Cooking time: 20 min
Serves 4

2 tbsp olive oil
200g chicken breast, skinned and finely diced
1 onion, chopped
1 garlic clove, chopped
2 stalks celery, chopped
300g button mushrooms, roughly chopped
1 tbsp chopped fresh thyme
1 tbsp dry sherry
700ml chicken stock
2 tbsp double cream
sprigs watercress, to serve

Pumpkin soup with crispy ham

1. Heat the oil in a large pan and add the onion. Cook until soft. Add the garlic and chilli and cook for 2 minutes.

2. Add the chopped pumpkin, stir for 1 minute, then add the stock and the tomatoes. Season with salt and pepper and simmer gently until the pumpkin is tender.

3. Blend to a smooth purée and serve in warmed bowls garnished with the fried ham or bacon.

Preparation time: 5 min
Cooking time: 35 min
Serves 4

3 tbsp oil
1 onion, finely chopped
1 garlic clove, chopped
1 red chilli, deseeded and chopped
450g pumpkin, peeled, deseeded and chopped
500ml vegetable stock
400g tinned tomatoes, chopped
2 slices Parma ham or bacon, fried until crisp

Low-fat fish chowder

1. Heat the oil in a large pan and gently cook the onion until soft but not brown. Add the garlic, cook for 1 minute and stir in the potatoes and the turmeric.

2. Cook for 2 minutes and add the stock. Bring to a boil and simmer gently for 20 minutes or until the potatoes are tender.

3. Add the fish, simmer for 3 minutes or until just cooked through, then season with salt and pepper.

4. Set aside about half the soup mixture and blend the remainder to a purée. Set aside 4 tablespoons of the yoghurt and stir the remaining into the purée.

5. Return the purée to the pan with the reserved mixture, reheat gently. Serve in warmed bowls garnished with the reserved yoghurt and a sprinkling of turmeric.

Preparation time: 10 min
Cooking time: 30 min
Serves 4

2 tbsp sunflower oil
1 onion, finely chopped
1 garlic clove, chopped
*3 medium potatoes, peeled
  and chopped*
2 tsp ground turmeric
800ml fish stock
450g cod fillet, cut into chunks
250ml low-fat yoghurt

Prawn and fennel chowder

Preparation time: 5 min
Cooking time: 30 min
Serves 4

2 tbsp butter
2 shallots, finely chopped
2 bulbs fennel, finely sliced
2 garlic cloves, chopped
2 tbsp pastis
750ml fish or vegetable stock
1 small sweet potato, chopped
450g prawns, shelled
125ml double cream
chilli powder, to serve

1. Heat the butter in a large pan and gently add the shallots. Cook until soft. Add the fennel and garlic, cook for 2 minutes then add the pastis and let it bubble.

2. Add the stock, bring to a boil then add the sweet potato and simmer gently for 20 minutes or until the sweet potato is tender.

3. Season with salt and pepper then stir in the prawns and cream. Simmer until the prawns are cooked through then serve in warmed bowls with a pinch of chilli powder sprinkled over.

Rose-hip soup

1. Place the rose hips, apple, salt and water in a large pan and bring to boil.

2. Simmer gently for 20–30 minutes or until the rose hips are tender. Blend to a purée and pass through a fine sieve into a clean pan.

3. Stir in the sugar, lemon juice and cornflour, reheat gently, then stir in the cream.

4. Serve with the toasted bread.

Preparation time: 5 min
Cooking time: 35 min
Serves 4

450g rose hips, washed
1 small apple, peeled, cored
  and chopped
pinch of salt
1 litre water
2 tbsp sugar
juice of 1 lemon
1 tbsp cornflour, mixed with a
  little water
75ml double cream
8–12 slices French bread,
  toasted

Parsnip soup

1. Toast the cumin seeds in a dry pan for 30 seconds and set aside.

2. Heat the oil in a large pan and gently add the onion and garlic. Cook until soft. Stir in the cumin seeds, reserving a few to garnish, and cook for 2 minutes.

3. Add the parsnips to the pan, stir well and add the stock or water. Bring to a boil and simmer gently for 20–25 minutes or until the parsnips are tender.

4. Blend to a smooth purée and return to the pan and season with salt and pepper. Pour into warmed bowls, stir in the cream and garnish with the reserved cumin seeds and a sprinkle of cayenne pepper.

Preparation time: 5 min
Cooking time: 35 min
Serves 4

2 tbsp cumin seeds
3 tbsp vegetable oil
1 onion, chopped
1 garlic clove, chopped
750g parsnips, peeled and chopped
750ml vegetable stock or water
125ml double cream
cayenne pepper, to serve

Tomato soup

1. Heat the oil in a large pan and gently add the onions. Fry until soft. Add the garlic and chilli pepper and cook for 2 more minutes.

2. Add the chopped tomatoes and tomato paste, and pour on the stock. Stir in the basil, parsley and balsamic vinegar. Season with salt, sugar and 1–2 dashes Tabasco.

3. Bring to a boil and simmer for 20–25 minutes, stirring occasionally.

4. Blend the soup until smooth then pass through a fine sieve into a clean pan. Reheat gently then stir in the crème fraîche and check the seasoning.

5. Serve in bowls, garnished with chopped chives and drizzled with a little oil.

Preparation time: 5 min
Cooking time: 30 min
Serves 4

3 tbsp olive oil
2 onions, chopped
2 garlic cloves, chopped
1 red chilli pepper, deseeded
   and chopped
400g tinned tomatoes, chopped
2 tbsp tomato paste
600ml vegetable stock
2 tbsp fresh basil, chopped
1 tbsp fresh parsley, chopped
3 tbsp balsamic vinegar
½ tsp sugar
Tabasco, to taste
4 tbsp crème fraîche
chopped chives and olive oil,
   to serve

Pea soup with basil

Preparation time: 5 min
Cooking time: 15 min
Serves 4

3 tbsp vegetable oil
1 onion, finely chopped
600g frozen peas
750ml vegetable stock
250ml double cream
basil leaves, to serve

1. Heat the oil in a large pan and add the onion. Cook until soft but not brown.

2. Add the peas and pour over the stock then bring to a boil and simmer for 10 minutes.

3. Add the cream and blend to a smooth purée. Season with salt and pepper, and reheat gently. Serve garnished with the basil leaves.

Beetroot soup

1. Heat the butter in a large pan and gently add the onion and garlic. Cook until soft but not brown.

2. Add the potatoes and beetroot, cook for 2 minutes then add the stock and the bay leaf. Bring to a boil and simmer gently until the vegetables are tender.

3. Remove the bay leaf then blend to a smooth purée. Add the vinegar and season with salt and pepper.

4. Mix the garnish ingredients together and serve with the soup.

Preparation time: 15 min
Cooking time: 25 min
Serves 4

3 tbsp butter
1 onion, finely chopped
1 garlic clove, chopped
2 medium potatoes, peeled and chopped
450g beetroot, peeled and chopped
1 litre vegetable or meat stock
1 bay leaf
2 tbsp red wine vinegar

To serve:
¼ cucumber, finely chopped
½ red onion, finely chopped
1 red chilli pepper, deseeded and finely chopped
2 tbsp olive oil

Butternut squash soup

1. Heat the oil in a pan and gently add the onion, garlic, ginger and chilli. Cook until soft.

2. Add the curry powder, cook for 1 minute then add the squash and the sugar and stir for 2 minutes until the squash begins to caramelise.

3. Add the stock, cover and cook gently for about 35 minutes or until the squash is very tender.

4. While the soup is cooking, make the croutons. Fry the bread in the butter until golden brown. Season with salt and pepper, then drain on kitchen paper.

5. When the soup is cooked, blend to a purée and add the orange juice and cream. Season with salt and pepper and reheat gently. Ladle the hot soup into bowls and serve garnished with thyme and croutons.

Preparation time: 15 min
Cooking time: 50 min
Serves 4

4 tbsp oil
1 onion, chopped
1 garlic clove, chopped
thumb-sized piece fresh ginger, peeled and chopped
1 red chilli, deseeded and chopped
1 tsp curry powder
800g butternut squash, peeled, deseeded and chopped
1 tbsp sugar
500ml vegetable stock
125ml orange juice
200ml double cream
Sprigs thyme, to serve

For the croutons:
2 slices stale white bread, cubed
2 tbsp butter

Making croutons

Croutons add a delicious crunch to dishes that need a bit of extra texture, and are most often used in salads and soups. It is the perfect way to use up any dry or stale leftover bread.

STEP 1 Cut the bread into slices using a sharp knife. and trim away the crust.

STEP 2 Cut the bread pieces into long, evenly sized strips using a sharp bread knife.

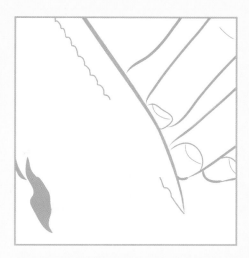

STEP 3 Cut across the bread strips to create bite-sized cubes, keeping them of a fairly uniform shape.

STEP 4 Heat some butter or vegetable oil in a frying pan. Add the croutons and cook until golden on all sides.

STEP 5 Remove from the pan using a slotted spoon and drain on kitchen paper. Add to soup just before serving.

New England clam chowder

1. Drain the clams, reserving the liquid, and set aside. Place the liquid in a measuring jug and add enough water to make the volume up to 750ml.

2. Heat the butter in a pan and gently add the bacon. Fry until lightly browned. Remove the bacon from the pan and set aside.

3. Place the onions and garlic in the pan and cook gently until soft but not brown. Return the bacon to the pan and scatter over the flour. Cook for 2 minutes, stirring all the time.

4. Gradually add the clam liquid, stirring all the time. Add the potatoes, thyme and bay leaf. Season with salt and pepper then simmer very gently until the potatoes are very tender. Add a little more water if needed.

5. Add the clams and cream, reheat very gently and serve in warmed bowls.

Preparation time: 15 min
Cooking time: 35 min
Serves 4

2 cans clams in water
1 tbsp butter
4 rashers bacon, chopped
2 onions, finely chopped
1 garlic cloves, finely chopped
2 tbsp flour
2 large potatoes, cut into cubes
1 tbsp thyme leaves
1 bay leaf
125ml double cream

Asparagus and potato soup with black truffle

1. Heat the butter in a large pan and gently add the onion. Cook until soft.

2. Add the potatoes and cook for 2 minutes. Add the stock and bring to the boil. Simmer until the potatoes are soft then add the asparagus, reserving a few asparagus tips to garnish.

3. Blend to a smooth purée then pass through a fine sieve into a clean pan. Season with salt and pepper, stir in the parsley and reheat gently.

4. Serve the soup in warmed bowls with the truffle shaved over and the reserved asparagus and chives on top.

Preparation time: 10 min
Cooking time: 35 min
Serves 4

3 tbsp butter
1 onion, finely chopped
2 medium potatoes, peeled and
*   finely chopped*
750ml chicken stock
2 cans white asparagus, drained
2 tbsp chopped parsley
1 black truffle, shaved, to serve
chopped chives, to serve

Tofu and cucumber miso soup

1. Heat the oil and gently add the garlic, spring onions and ginger. Cook for 2 minutes. Add the cucumber, then add the stock, miso paste and soy sauce. Simmer for about 4 minutes.

2. Season with lemon juice, salt and pepper. Pour into warmed bowls and serve with the tofu, coriander and cayenne pepper sprinkled over.

Preparation time: 15 min
Cooking time: 6 min
Serves 4

3 tbsp oil
1 garlic clove, finely chopped
1 bunch spring onions, sliced into rings
thumb-sized piece fresh ginger, peeled and grated
1 cucumber, seeds removed, roughly chopped
500ml vegetable stock
2 tbsp light miso paste
2 tbsp light soy sauce
1 tbsp lemon juice
250g tofu, diced, to serve
2 tbsp fresh coriander, finely chopped, to serve
pinch cayenne pepper, to serve

Chicken mulligatawny soup

Preparation time: 10 min
Cooking time: 45 min
Serves 4

3 tbsp ghee or vegetable oil
2 garlic cloves, chopped
1 tsp fresh ginger, peeled
  and grated
1 tsp ground caraway
1 tsp ground coriander
1 tsp curry powder
1 tsp turmeric
1l chicken stock
200g red lentils, rinsed
2 chicken breasts, chopped into
  1cm chunks
cayenne pepper
grated nutmeg
1 tbsp lemon juice
1 tbsp coriander leaves,
  roughly chopped, to serve

1. Heat the ghee in a pan and add the garlic and ginger. Gently fry until soft. Add the caraway, coriander, curry powder and turmeric and fry for 2 minutes.

2. Pour on the stock and add the lentils. Bring to a boil and simmer over a low heat for about 30 minutes or until the lentils are very soft. Stir occasionally.

3. Blend to a coarse purée and add the chicken. Simmer gently for about 10 minutes or until the chicken is cooked through.

4. Season with salt, cayenne pepper, nutmeg and lemon juice. Stir in the coriander leaves and serve.

Carrot soup

1. Heat the oil in a large pan and gently add the garlic, ginger and curry powder. Cook for 30 seconds.

2. Add the carrots and potatoes, stir for 2 minutes and add the stock. Bring to a boil then simmer gently until the vegetables are very tender.

3. Blend to a smooth purée and pass through a fine sieve into a clean pan. Add most of the cream, reserving a little to garnish, season with salt and pepper and reheat gently.

4. Pour into warmed bowls and serve with a swirl of the remaining cream and the chopped parsley.

Preparation time: 10 min
Cooking time: 30 min
Serves 4

3 tbsp vegetable oil
2 garlic cloves, chopped
thumb-sized piece fresh ginger,
* peeled and chopped*
1 tsp curry powder
450g carrots, chopped
2 medium potatoes, chopped
750ml vegetable stock
250ml double cream
1 tbsp chopped parsley

Roasted cream of tomato and basil soup

1. Heat the oven to 400°F (200°C). Place the tomatoes, onion and garlic in a large roasting tin, season with salt and freshly ground black pepper and drizzle with the olive oil. Roast for 20 minutes, then pour over the hot stock. Return to the oven and cook for 20 minutes or until the tomatoes are soft.

2. Meanwhile place the crème fraîche and basil in a food processor and blend until the basil is finally chopped.

3. Pour the soup in batches into a food processor or liquidiser and blend until smooth.

4. Place in a large saucepan, reheat gently, and stir in the basil cream.

Preparation time: 10 min
Cooking time: 1 h
Serves 4

1kg ripe tomatoes, halved
1 large red onion, sliced
1 garlic clove, peeled
1 tbsp olive oil
1 litre hot vegetable stock
200ml crème fraîche
large handful fresh basil

Smoked haddock chowder

1. Melt the butter in a large pan and add the onion. Cook for 3 minutes. Add the bacon and cook for a further 3 minutes until browned.

2. Add the milk and stock, stir in the potatoes then bring to the boil. Season well with freshly ground black pepper, cover and simmer for 10 minutes, or until the potatoes are tender.

3. Stir in the sweetcorn and add the haddock. Cover and simmer gently for 4–5 minutes, or until the fish starts to flake. Stir in the spinach and serve with crusty bread.

Preparation time: 10 min
Cooking time: 25 min
Serves 4

25g unsalted butter
1 onion, chopped
4 rashers smoked back bacon, chopped
450ml semi-skimmed milk
300ml fish stock
225g potatoes, peeled and cut into 1cm cubes
1 x 195g tin sweetcorn, drained
450g undyed smoked haddock fillet, skinned and cut into chunks
100g baby spinach leaves

Spring vegetable pistou

Preparation time: 15 min
Cooking time: 25 min
Serves 4

30ml olive oil
1 onion, chopped
1 garlic clove, crushed
600ml vegetable stock
300g baby new potatoes, halved
350g baby carrots, peeled
200g baby courgettes, halved
  lengthways
4 tomatoes, chopped
150g garden peas
150g broad beans, skins removed

For the pistou:
4 garlic cloves
30 fresh basil leaves
120ml extra virgin olive oil
50g Parmesan cheese, grated

1. Heat the oil in a large saucepan and add the onion and garlic. Cook for 2–3 minutes, until softened. Pour over the stock, bring to the boil and add the potatoes. Cover and simmer for 10 minutes.

2. Stir in the carrots, courgette and tomatoes, cover and simmer for 10 minutes. Add the peas and broad beans and cook for 4–5 minutes, until tender. Season to taste.

3. Meanwhile, make the pistou: place the garlic and basil in a food processor and blend to a paste, gradually add the olive oil, then stir in the Parmesan.

4. Ladle the soup into bowls and serve each with a spoonful of the pistou and crusty bread.

Thai green curry prawn soup

1. Heat the oil in a large pan and add the shallots and garlic. Fry until softened. Stir in the curry paste and cook for 1 minute, then add the coconut milk, stock and lemongrass.

2. Simmer, uncovered, for 10 minutes, then add the fish sauce, green beans and red pepper. Cook for 5 minutes then stir in the prawns. Simmer for 2–3 minutes until the prawns are heated through.

3. Serve in bowls scattered with the coriander and with a wedge of lime to squeeze over.

Preparation time: 5 min
Cooking time: 20 min
Serves 4

1 tbsp olive oil
2 shallots, finely chopped
1 garlic clove, crushed
2 tbsp Thai Green curry paste
400ml can coconut milk
450ml fish stock
2 stalks lemongrass, roughly chopped
2 tsp fish sauce
100g green beans, sliced
1 red pepper, thinly sliced
250g peeled and cooked tiger prawns
2 tbsp freshly chopped coriander, to serve
fresh lime wedges, to serve

Watercress soup

1. Melt the butter in alarge pan and add the onion, leek and potatoes. Cook gently for 5 minutes, stirring occasionally.

2. Stir in the watercress, stock and seasoning, cover and simmer for 10 minutes, stirring occasionally.

3. Place in a food processor or blender and blend until smooth. Add the milk.

4. Return to the pan, heat through, then ladle into bowls and garnish with the sprigs of watercress and freshly ground black pepper.

Preparation time: 10 min
Cooking time: 15 min
Serves 4

25g butter
1 onion, chopped
1 small leek, thinly sliced
2 medium potatoes, peeled and diced
225g watercress, roughly chopped, plus extra sprigs to serve
850ml chicken stock
150ml milk

Index